Books by F. N. Monjo

The Drinking Gourd
Grand Papa and Ellen Aroon
Indian Summer
The Jezebel Wolf
King George's Head Was Made of Lead
Ma and Willie and Pa
The One Bad Thing About Father
Pirates in Panama
Poor Richard in France
Rudi and the Distelfink
The Sea Beggar's Son
The Secret of the Sachem's Tree
Slater's Mill
The Vicksburg Veteran

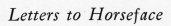

Letters to Horseface

Letters to Horseface

being the story of
Wolfgang Amadeus Mozart's
journey to Italy
1769-1770
when he was a boy of fourteen

❦

by F. N. Monjo
illustrated & designed by
Don Bolognese &
Elaine Raphael

The Viking Press · New York

First Edition
Text copyright © 1975 by Ferdinand Monjo and Louise L. Monjo
Illustrations copyright © 1975 by Don Bolognese and Elaine Raphael
All rights reserved
First published in 1975 by The Viking Press, Inc.
625 Madison Avenue, New York, N. Y. 10022
Published simultaneously in Canada by
The Macmillan Company of Canada Limited
Printed in U.S.A.
1 2 3 4 5 79 78 77 76 75

Library of Congress Cataloging in Publication Data

Monjo, F N
Letters to Horseface, being the story of Wolfgang
Amadeus Mozart's journey to Italy, 1769–1770, when he
was a boy of fourteen.

Bibliography: p.
SUMMARY: While journeying through Italy in 1770,
fourteen-year-old Mozart relates his experiences in
letters to his sister.
1. Mozart, Johann Chrysostom Wolfgang Amadeus,
1756–1791—Juvenile fiction. 2. Berchtold zu Sonnenburg, Maria Anna (Mozart) Reichsfreiin von, 1751–1829—
Juvenile fiction. [1. Mozart, Johann Chrysostom
Wolfgang Amadeus, 1756–1791—Fiction. 2. Berchtold
zu Sonnenburg, Maria Anna (Mozart) Reichsfreiin von
1751–1829—Fiction. 3. Italy—Fiction] I. Bolognese,
Don, ill. II. Raphael, Elaine, ill. III. Title.
PZ7.M75Le   [Fic]   74-23766
ISBN 0–670–42738–1

To the memory of
Lony Warinka Lyman
and
Arthur N. Bowen, Jr.,
who taught me how to listen
to Mozart
thirty and forty years ago,
long before I ever dreamed
of writing anything about him
F. N. M.

To our friends in Italy
Paola and Fred Caronna
Mary and Dom Grasso
for their love and pasta
April 1972
E. R. & D. B.

Salzburg

Wörgl
Innsbruck

SWITZERLAND

AUSTRIA

Brixen
Bozen

Trent
Roveredo

FRANCE

Milan
Lodi

Verona
Padua
Mantua
Parma

Venice

YUGOSLAVIA

Bologna

Florence

Sinegaglia
Loreto

ADRIATIC SEA

ITALY

Rome

Teopold and
Wolfgang Mozart's
travels to Italy

December 12, 1769 — March 28, 1771

——————— Going
- - - - - - - Return

Naples

N
W   E
S

CONTENTS

INNSBRUCK

Dear Nannerl—

How is Mama? And how are you, my dear Horseface? I suppose I should say: *cara sorella mia.*

Do you know what that means? "Cara" is dear; and "sorella" is sister; so, it's "my dear little sister." You see, I've been studying Italian!

Papa says we'll be in Italy soon enough, so he practices speaking Italian with me every evening.

You won't believe it, but ever since we left you and Mama in Salzburg, three days ago, I've been wishing both of you could have come with us. I know Papa says traveling is *expensive.* But I wish Mama and my dear sister, Nannerl-the-Horseface, could have come along on our trip, anyway.

You should have seen the Alps before we came into Innsbruck this afternoon! They were glittering with ice. And all the branches of the fir trees were bowed down under loads of powdery snow. The Alps, in our Austrian Tyrol, rise up steep—stark white and silver—against a blue, blue sky, like a cathedral organ ready to burst into a hymn to God. And at sunset, everything turns from silver and white to rosy pink.

Our coachman was a very careful driver, so Papa calmed down, and trusted him enough to get some sleep. The horses were fast and lively. And, as you know, there's nothing your little brother likes better than a fast coach ride! So I stayed wide awake.

As we passed through a tiny mountain village, the chimes were ringing out the hour. Just the notes you'd expect:

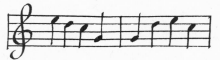

They were such delicate, silvery notes that I thought, someday Wolferl, you must remember to write a little something for bells. Sleighbells, maybe. Or chimes. Or the glockenspiel!

Then a pretty little melody came capering and dancing into my head, almost a counterpoint to the horses' hooves and to Papa Leopold's snoring. I thought the phrases out, to the end, then went back and added the bass accompaniment, and popped it all back into my memory bag. Who knows when I may need it? When I *do* need it, here it will be, just as good as new. Up here, safe in my silly head!

Papa says I must be very serious, and work harder than ever, in Italy. I must use my eyes and ears and learn *everything* there is to learn, about music. Operas, especially.

Papa says, "Remember, Wolferl, we are not traveling to Italy on holiday. We have no time for nonsense. Italy is the school of music for all Europe. And so we are going to *learn*. We must show these Italians what a fine, accomplished musician you are, even if you are only thirteen. And if we are lucky, they will ask you to write a full-scale opera for the duke's opera house in Milan, or for the San Carlo opera, in Naples."

Poor Papa! Nothing but business, business, business. You know what he's like. I just smile and nod and keep making jokes and composing bits and scraps of melodies for my memory bag. One of the melodies I wrote today, Nannerl, makes me think of you. It *sounds* like you, if you know what I mean. And it makes me think of your smile. It might make a pretty rondo. . . .

Oh, I meant to ask you. Are you practicing at the harpsi-

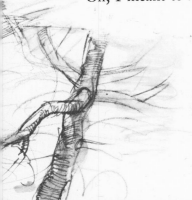

chord every day, as you promised Papa you would? And are you taking care not to sing so much that you hurt your throat? And do you still gossip all afternoon with your lady friends, Waberl and Sallerl? And is our landlord, Herr Hagenauer, still able to make you blush when he teases you about Anton von Molk? And what about Anton himself? Are you still kissing him behind Mama's back? Are you, Horseface? Tra-la-la-liera! Tra-la-la-liera! I feel sure you are. (Unless Nannerl-the-flirt has replaced him with somebody new.)

I'm sleepy and I should go to bed. We're in a comfortable inn, here in Innsbruck. But I wish I were back at No. 9 Getreidegasse, on the Löchelplatz, in Salzburg. Home with you and Mama and Papa. There we would have just finished our nice hot supper of liver dumplings and sauerkraut. And then Herr Schactner would come by, and he and Papa would tune up their violins. And Deible would come puffing upstairs with his oboe. And Leutgeb would close up his cheese-shop and come to our apartment lugging his French horn. And Mama and I would sit at the harpsichord. And we'd begin our little evening concert—our *kleine nachtmusik*—and maybe, if we asked politely, and begged, maybe Nannerl-the-Horseface herself would sing! Tra-la-la-liera! Tra-la-la-liera!

Now Papa has just called out "Wolferl, time for bed!" So I must say my prayers, and blow out the candle, and obey him. You know, I always used to say: "After God, comes Papa." And I still say it yet.

Papa says please ask Mama not to forget to tell our boss, Archbishop Schrattenbach, that the Mighty Musical Mozarts will not linger in Italy one moment longer than necessary. He says to say that we will be back in Salzburg in a year *at the latest,* ready to write thousands of masses and oratorios for the Archbishop's chapel, and ready to put on millions of concerts for his courtiers.

But if I know Papa, my dear Horseface, you won't see either of us Mighty Musical Mozarts again until after your booby brother Wolferl has written an opera for *somebody,* down there in sunny Italy! Not if I know Papa Leopold!

But I mustn't stop without asking about Miss Bimbes! How is my dear little dog? Does she miss me? Does she still howl and chase her tail when you trill your high B-flat? Give that Bimberl a kiss or two on the nose for me. And a wine biscuit. And a pat on her glossy behind. And a scratch behind her ear.

And give Mama 10,000 kisses from me. And save a few for yourself, from . . .

Your silly little brother with the great big name:
Johann Chrysostom Wolfgang Amadeus Mozart,
more briefly known to his family as,
Wolferl.

P.S. Papa brought the key to the clavichord away with him, by mistake, and is sending it back to you.

W.

MANTUA

January 18, 1770

Dear Nannerl-the-Horseface,

It's been more than a month since I wrote a whole letter to you, of your very own. But I have been so busy, and so much has happened, that you must forgive me.

Did Papa tell you anything about Innsbruck? The mountains were so high, there, they seemed to hang right over the buildings in the town. And there was a triumphal arch, built five years ago, when our most gracious Empress Maria Theresa's son, Archduke Leopold, married the Infanta Maria Luisa of Spain. (Papa says Archduke Leopold is now the grand duke of Tuscany. He lives in Florence, and we may see him when we visit there.)

From Innsbruck, we traveled through the Brenner Pass, between high, high ranges of the Alps, and then passed through the towns of Steinach, and Brizen, and Bozen, to

14

Trent. Trent is an old walled town that fills the whole valley.

We were in Roveredo on December 24. And on Christmas Day (Mama's birthday!) I played the organ in the church, there. So many people came to hear me that a couple of strong fellows had to push some of the people aside so that I could get into the choir. Two days after that we were in the old Italian town of Verona, staying at an inn called The Sign of the Two Towers. Do you know what that is, in Italian, Horseface? It's *Due Torre*.

Verona is a lovely town, on a rushing river called the Adige. Papa says this is where Romeo and Juliet lived.

Everyone in the streets of Verona was wearing masks when we were there, because Carnival had begun. I wish you could have seen the floats that were pulled through the streets by horses decorated with ribbons and flowers. And the costumes! Dozens of Pulcinellos in white smocks and masks and floppy gray hats. Gay Harlequins in red and yellow suits, with bells on their caps. And girls dressed as soldiers with epaulettes, or wearing pretty Columbina costumes. All of them dancing in the streets, or lining the balconies and crowding the windows, throwing flowers and streamers and bonbons and confetti and gilded chocolates and silver and copper coins into the crowd. The Italians go *mad* at Carnival time!

They have horse races by day, and plays and balls and fireworks at night. Quite enough to make Nannerl-the-flirt as happy as can be.

16

I can't tell you how many melodies I put down safely into my memory bag, in Verona. One for a Harlequin that I think should be bright and silvery when played on the flute. Several for fireworks. And something just right for a lovely young girl, just beginning to fall in love. . . .

The best thing about Carnival time is this: you don't have to be polite. You can talk to anyone you want. You don't have to be introduced to anyone, or call them by name, because everybody's incognito, wearing a mask, anyhow! "*Servitore umilissimo, Signora Maschera,*" you say. Know what *that* means, Horseface? It means "your most humble servant,

Masked Lady." Doesn't that sound like fun? Just think what *you* might do in a crowd of maskers, Nannerl. Someday, I've promised myself, I'm going to write something in an opera, for people at a masked ball. I'm as *sure* of it as anything!

Good old business-like Papa Leopold has taken care to have letters of introduction with him, addressed to all the important people in Italy. So we find friends ready to help us wherever we go. That's why Signor Locatelli took us out in his carriage to see the huge old Roman amphitheater, while we were in Verona.

And we gave another organ concert in the church, and everybody came crowding to see "the little organist." And guess what? While I was there, in Verona, Papa said I had to sit for my portrait. I wore my diamond ring on the little finger of my right hand. And the artist painted me in my wig and my new red velvet suit with the gold braid trim. I was shown just turning away from the harpsichord, as if I were the *dearest* little angel. As if butter wouldn't melt in my mouth. You would laugh, Nannerl, to see the ridiculously innocent expression your brother Wolferl has on his innocent little mug! Papa *adores* the picture, but I know you and Mama will laugh when you see it—because that's what *I* wanted to do!

And then from Verona we came straight down to Mantua, where we are now, staying at the Sign of the Croce Verde— the Green Cross to you, Horseface.

Don't believe anything they tell you about "sunny Italy," Nannerl. It's *cold* here in winter. Cold! Cold! Cold! If Papa hadn't bought us two foot-bags lined with fur, our feet would have frozen in the carriage—in spite of the hay we put down on the floor of the coach. My face is chapped a reddish-brown from the cold—plus the fact that it gets scorched from the heat of the inn fire, whenever I come in from outside. (I'm only joking. Don't let Mama take me seriously and start worrying.)

Two days ago, on January 16, I gave a public concert here in Mantua, at the Accademia Filarmonica (the Philharmonic Academy to you, Horseface). The Italians think I'm a lot younger than thirteen—but Papa doesn't mind that a bit! I'm so small I must look as if I'm only nine or ten, I suppose. But you and Mama know I'll be *fourteen* in a few days —on January 27. Sh-h-h-h! Let's keep it a secret.

Anyway, the concert was a big success, and Papa was happy because he was able to take in some gold pieces at the door, to offset the huge amount we've been spending. ("Money doesn't grow on trees, Wolferl," says Papa Leopold.)

You and Mama would laugh if you could hear what they *call* me. In Germany and Austria, when I was little, they used to call me the *wunderkind*—the "wonder-child." You remember? Well, the Italians can't say Wolfgang. Or Johann. Or Chrysostom. Or wunderkind, either, for that matter. So they call me Amadeo. That's right. They call me the *es-*

pertissimo giovanetto, Signor Amadeo. (For your benefit, my dear Nannerl, that means: "that most accomplished youth, Signor Amadeus." That's *me*, your brother Wolferl, they're referring to!)

And here's what that "most accomplished youth" did at his concert, Horseface:

1. Conducted a symphony of his own composition.
2. Improvised a harpsichord sonata, with variations—composed right then and there.
3. Composed and sang an aria to words given to him on the spot—never before seen by him.
4. Composed a fugue and variations on a theme given to him (and seen by him for the first time) in the concert hall.
5. Performed on the violin, in a string trio, in which he had to improvise his part.

So you see, Papa is still up to his old tricks! It's not enough for me to be simply a good musician. Or a good composer. I must still do tricks and improvisations to surprise the donkey's ears, in the audience.

Of course, it's not as bad as it was eight years ago—when I was about six and you were eleven—when Papa Leopold and Mama showed us off, the first time, in Vienna, to Emperor Francis and Empress Maria Theresa. Will you ever forget it, Nannerl? Such nonsense! They discovered I had perfect pitch, and some fool lady would tinkle her spoon

against her champagne glass and say "What note is this, my dear little Wolfgang? My adorable little wunderkind?" And I would have to answer, "That is F-sharp, your ladyship." And then a fat gentleman would ring the little chime on his pocket watch, and ask me to tell him what note *that* was. And I would have to reply, "That is E-flat, Prince Unterschlossberg. E-flat, without a doubt!"

And the ladies would kiss, and kiss, and *kiss* me, and the gentlemen would say "Astounding! *Wunderbar!* Unheard of! *Unglaublich!* Unbelievable!"

Even the emperor wasn't content to let me play my sonatas on the harpsichord, and be done with it. For, when I was finished, he would make us cover the keyboard with a cloth—do you remember? And Papa would look so pleased when I was able to play my sonata, without any mistakes, even with

sitting for my portrait in Verona

the keyboard hidden! And then Empress Maria Theresa would take me up onto her fat lap and kiss me some more, and tell Papa I was a wonder. "A wunderkind, Herr Mozart! A wunderkind such as the world has never seen before!"

It was all very tiresome. Most of them didn't want to hear me play. Not really. They preferred to see me do my tricks, like a little monkey.

Now Papa says I'm much too old for any more tricks of that kind. "You're much too old to play the wunderkind in Italy, Wolferl," he says. But he *still* lets them give me melodies to improvise, and things like that, at my concerts.

Maybe someday, Nannerl, my music will be enough. Do you suppose that day will ever come?

While here, in Mantua, we've been to the opera. The prima donna was old, and not very good-looking, but she didn't have a bad voice. The opera was by Papa's friend, Herr Hasse. And the tenor had a beautiful voice. I forget his name.

Sometime I must tell you how noisy and talkative the Italians are when they go to the opera. They're much worse than the audience in Vienna!

Papa says the post is ready to leave, so I'll have to stop. Kiss Mama 10,000 times for me, and save a few for yourself.

Your brother,
Wolfgang, in Austria, but
Amadeo in Italy!

MILAN

March 3, 1770

Dear Nannerl-the-flirt,

Have you been kissing Anton lately? Or is it Hans by now? Or Fritz? Or Karl? Be sure to write and tell me. Papa and I love getting letters from you and Mama. When the post from Austria arrives, and there are letters from Salzburg for us, that night, at dinner, my appetite is better. Even Papa has noticed.

This is the last day of Carnival, here in Milan. Tomorrow, Lent begins. So there will be a huge parade and balls and fireworks tonight, but at the stroke of midnight, all the merry-making will come to an end.

Papa had letters of introduction to Count Carl von Firmian, here. He is the governor of Lombardy. He had a very bad cold, and couldn't see us when we first arrived. But now he is going to give a big concert for me, on the twelfth. The archbishop of Milan will be there, and the duke of Modena, and his daughter, and all the important people in Milan.

Papa and I have ordered new cloaks and new suits (mine is a blue taffeta, lined with rose; Papa's is brown, lined with yellow) for the concert. Papa says this is expensive tomfoolery, but one *has* to look well-dressed before the nobility.

We have gone several times to the opera here. Once, wearing masks! I promised you in my last letter that I would tell you how the Italians behave at the opera, and so I will.

You know how noisy people are—how they flirt and laugh and talk during the performance, in Vienna? It is even *worse* here in Italy! Can you believe it? Well, it is true.

First of all, in Milan, even though they know all the old operas very well indeed, many people keep coming every night, no matter how many times they've heard the opera before. If it is a *new* opera, they may quiet down and listen to the whole thing. But if it is an old opera, the audience is talking the whole time, hushing (they say, *"Zitti! Zitti!"* when they want people to hush) only when the singers come to a favorite beautiful aria. Venders go through the pit, calling out, selling ices and fruit. In the boxes, card tables are set up. You can hear the click of dice and the shuffling of

they hardly ever stop talking at the Opera!

cards. Everybody up there is gambling. Sometimes the gentlemen spit down into the pit, where their servants are sitting! Some of the boxes even have mirrors on the rear walls, so the card players don't have to interrupt their gambling in order to see the singers and dancers on stage! In a few boxes, they have small stoves, for cooking food. Ladies and gentlemen call and smile from one box to the other, hardly ever seeming to look at the stage.

You would think—with so much uproar—that the singers would never make themselves heard. But they do! Over all of it, the music soars and floats. And when the Italians *like* a singer, they *really* love him! "Bravo! Bravissimo!" they call, and they drown the house with applause. Then they go back to their cards and fruit.

Papa has taken me to some rehearsals, too. For the great Niccolò Piccini is here this season, getting his opera, *Caesar and Cleopatra*, ready for opening night. Papa wanted me to meet him, and to hear his work. So I did.

I also met old Maestro Giovanni Sammartini, who is the director of half of all the church choirs in Milan. Papa wanted me to play him a new aria I had written—and when Sammartini had heard me sing it, he said, "Herr Mozart, this boy must write an opera for us, himself! He is astonishing! A marvel! Astounding!"

Maestro Sammartini told the director of the opera all about me. And the director asked Papa if I would like to

"A marvel!"

write an opera for Milan, for next Christmas! What do you think of that, Nannerl?

Papa said, "Marvelous." But when we were back at the inn he whispered to me, privately, "Don't get your hopes up, Wolferl. I'll believe he means it *only* after I've seen the *scrittura*." (The scrittura, darling Horseface, is the contract.)

Well, wouldn't it be nice if I should chance to write an opera, and it were a big success? Then we could all be rich, and all of us could live happily in Salzburg, together again.

Papa is writing to Mama, so I will just send her 10,000 kisses, together with a hundred kisses or so for your own wonderful horseface, from,

Your simpleton brother,
Wolferl

CBOLOGNA

March 27, 1770

Cara sorella mia—

Do you remember what that means, Nannerl? "My dear little sister."

Look where we've got to, by now! We're in the old university town of Bologna, where Italy's oldest university is to be found. Maybe *Europe's* oldest university, for all I know! Anyway, Papa says it's 700 years old, and that three of Italy's greatest poets—Dante, Petrarch, and Tasso—studied here.

First I must tell you that before I left Milan, Count Firmian gave your young buffoon of a brother a going-away gift of a gold snuffbox, stuffed full of twenty gold pieces. I was pleased, and so was Papa—because we're not making as much money on this trip as we did the time all of us made the Grand Tour to Paris and London, seven years ago. Papa is right. I'm no longer the little trained-monkey wunderkind I used to be, and so the golden rain doesn't fall as heavily upon us as it did in the old days.

Tra-la-la-liera! Tra-la-la-liera! I refuse to worry or to be downhearted. I'd rather think about composing something lovely for woodwinds. You know, Horseface, sometimes I think the clarinet is the most beautiful instrument of them all? Unless it's the flute. Or the violin.

Anyway, we left Milan on March 15, traveling in a *vettura*. A vettura, my dear sorella, is a mule train, with armed guards carrying muskets. You know why we travel this way? Because there are bandits on the roads!

"Your money or your life!"

Bandits! Bandits with black hats and black mustaches, and black cloaks pulled up under their chins! Bandits ready to steal your gold and cut your throat, my little Nannerl! What do you think of that?

I've got a melody stored away in my memory bag, just right for a man in a black cloak. A sort-of-an-*almost*-bandit melody, you might say. You can hear the cloak swirling about in it, anyway. Someday I'll put it in an opera. Papa doesn't believe me, but then, Papa doesn't know everything.

That same day, March 15, we got to a town called Lodi. That night, at the inn, I began writing my first string quartet. You know, sometimes, Nannerl, I think the loveliest instrument in the world must be the cello. The piece is finished, now. Papa says it's a rather good quartet.

We went on to Parma, and there we met the celebrated young soprano, Lucrezia Agujari. I wish you could have heard her sing, Nannerl! Her trills and her incredibly high top notes, so pure and silvery. It made me realize that the most beautiful instrument of all, without a doubt, must be the human voice. Remind me to write an aria sometime for someone who can sing like Signorina Lucrezia Agujari.

After Parma we went by way of Modena to Bologna, arriving here three days ago, on the 24th. As we go farther south, Italy grows warmer and more springlike. Papa and I are happy to have left the winter behind us at last.

The day we got here, the scrittura—the contract—for the

opera was delivered to us, so it looks as if I *will* be writing the first opera for the Christmas season, in Milan, after all. I was almost as happy as Papa.

Yesterday evening, Count Pallavicini had a concert for me, to which 150 guests were invited. All of the notables from the university and all the nobility from around about Bologna attended.

The man Papa most wanted me to meet was Padre Martini. He came early, and stayed until the very end. He is about sixty-five, and a Franciscan monk. His face is kindly, and he wears a little black biretta. He applauded heartily when he heard me play and improvise. He told Papa that I was, "Very talented! Amazing!" And Papa asked him questions about what he should do with me, and with my career, just as if I were a piece of furniture there in the room, who couldn't hear what they were saying. You know Papa!

Papa says Padre Martini is writing a great history of music, and that he knows more about music and counterpoint

"Amazing," said Padre Martini — Bologna

than anybody else in all Europe. Everybody who cares about musical scholarship comes to Italy to try to meet Padre Martini. He is the most important member of the Bologna Philharmonic Academy. And Papa began telling him, right away, that he was the author of *The Violinist's Handbook*. Padre Martini hadn't read Papa's book, but he'd heard of it. Papa was so pleased! Now, Papa's writing Mama, asking her to send him a copy of the *Handbook*, because he wants to give a copy to Padre Martini, with a fancy inscription. You know Papa!

Now Papa says that Padre Martini is telling everybody he meets what a wonder I am. What a marvel! So it looks as if the Mighty Musical Mozarts are to be famous throughout Italy, after all.

Papa says, "If Martini says you're a genius, Wolferl, your reputation is *made!*"

But I just shake my head and smile, and go on composing melodies for my memory bag.

Poor Papa! Always so hard at work!

I went to visit Padre Martini again, yesterday, and composed a fugue for him. I think he liked it a lot. He walked with me in his garden and told me that many musicians, much older than I, would give anything to be able to write a fugue so rapidly and skillfully.

"You have a great gift, my dear little Signor Amadeo," said Padre Martini.

We were sitting in his grape arbor, and the leaves were just beginning to unfurl on the vines. The afternoon sunshine was warm.

"Yes, a great gift. A precious gift. You must give thanks to God for it, you know. And foster it. And be happy because He has bestowed it upon you. Do you understand me?"

"Well, Padre," I answered him, "that will be easy to do, for I am always happy when I am busy with my music." Then he smiled, and we went back inside, where Papa was waiting.

Padre Martini told Papa that I had a great future in music. And Papa looked very serious, and asked many questions about what he should do to forward my talent. And they talked together for a long time—sometimes in whispers—looking very worried, as if I had some terrible disease. What do you think of that, Nannerl?

And tomorrow we're going to visit the singer, Farinelli, at his villa. Papa says he's a famous opera singer, who used to sing all over Italy and then went to live in Madrid, at the court of the king of Spain.

My next letter will be from Florence, my dear Horseface, where we hope to be within the next three or four days.

Kisses (times 10,000) for you and Mama

from your Simple Simon brother,
Wolferl

FLORENCE

Dear Nannerl—

We are not going to be staying very long in Florence, because Papa wants to get to Rome in time for us to attend the solemn services during Holy Week at St. Peter's.

Just imagine! The cathedral in Salzburg is built to *imitate* the architecture of St. Peter's, in Rome, but by Eastertime, I shall have seen the *real thing*.

I must tell you about our drive from Bologna to Florence. It took us nearly four days, because you have to travel through the mountains—the Apennines. I wouldn't have minded that, except it was so windy and rainy that I caught a bad cold.

As soon as we got to Florence, we put up at the Sign of the Aquila (the Eagle, dear Horseface) and Papa made me take tea for my cold, along with violet juice, as medicine.

Florence is a beautiful city, you know, spread out around

its Duomo, or cathedral. All its buildings stretch along both banks of the Arno River, and all the rooftops are made of orange tiles. As soon as you cross the mountains from Bologna and begin coming down the southern slopes into Florence, you begin to see, for the first time, the tall dark pointed cypress trees, and the low, bushy, silvery-green olives.

We've met a lot of important people here, and I've made

a friend. I'll get the important people out of the way *first*, and then tell you about my friend. How's that?

The ambassador from Vienna, Count von Rosenberg, gave a concert for me, and the grand duke of Tuscany and his wife attended. As I told you before, the grand duke is our Empress Maria Theresa's son, the Archduke Leopold, whom you and I met seven or eight years ago when we were little children, in Vienna. He remembered *you*, Nannerl, and asked for you.

Archduke Leopold

And he remembered me, too. He laughed when he recalled the time his sister, the little Archduchess Marie Antoinette, helped pick me up when I slipped and fell on the waxed parquet floor of the palace. She was the only one to run and help me, and Archduke Leopold says that I told the empress that, because of what she had done for me, someday I would marry the little Marie Antoinette! Do you remember that? I had forgotten.

At the same concert, I also met Count Kaunitz, who is our empress's ambassador in Naples. And also the Marchese di Ligniville, who is the musical director here at court, and who knows almost as much about counterpoint as does Padre Martini, in Bologna.

Ligniville gave me the most difficult musical problems to solve—but I was able to take care of them quite rapidly. At least, that's what Papa says. Everyone seemed to be amazed and delighted.

But I haven't told you about the people I enjoyed meeting most. They were Maestro Nardini, and his young pupil, Thomas Linley.

You may remember Maestro Nardini. Papa says we heard him play the violin in Ludwigsburg, seven years ago when we were on our Grand Tour. Papa still says it would be impossible to hear a finer player for beauty, purity, evenness of tone, and singing quality—and coming from Herr Leopold, author of *The Violinist's Handbook*, that is praise indeed. But Papa is right. Signor Nardini plays beautifully. He accompanied me on the violin as I played some improvisations on the harpsichord. Tears sometimes run down onto his violin as he plays. Papa says Nardini is very kind and tenderhearted. He has just come here to Florence. Up until a month ago he was living in Leghorn, caring for his old master, the great virtuoso violinist Tartini, during the old man's final illness. Papa says Tartini played so incredibly well that people used to say he had taken lessons from the Devil himself! And not only that, Nannerl, he once wrote a violin sonata that they call *The Devil's Trill*.

But it is about his pupil, the English boy, Thomas Linley, that I must tell you. Thomas is a great virtuoso violinist. He is no older than your brother Wolferl, and he is a most accomplished violinist, or else the great Nardini wouldn't bother to give him lessons. The Italians call him Tomasso. His father is an Englishman who gives concerts and teaches singing at Bath. Papa says Tom is a real wunderkind, just like me! He says everybody in Italy is talking about us two boys.

I don't know about that part. All I know is that Tom Linley is a better violinist than I am. I've promised to write to him, and I hope to see him again. I hope you will meet him, too. I *know* you would like him.

This letter is not written in my usual beautiful handwriting (ha!) because I've had to use one of my musical notation pens, instead of a regular quill pen. So my writing is a little worse than usual. Anyway, Papa says it's time for me to stop and come to bed. So I will.

The next time you hear from us, we'll probably be in Rome.

Your dear little Italian brother,
Wolferl

P.S. Kiss Mama's hand for me, 10,000 times.

P.P.S. Tommasino Linley and I are now the best of friends. One night we took turns playing the violin at a concert for the gentry, and we kept it up all evening long. And the next day, he brought his violin to our rooms and played the whole afternoon for me and Papa. He and I played the violin again, in turn, the following afternoon—"not like boys, but like *men!*" said Papa. We have promised to write to each other.

And yesterday, when Tommasino learned that the Mighty Musical Mozarts were leaving for Rome, he burst into tears. And so did I. When Papa told him we would not be departing until noon, today, he promised to come say good-by to us. Sure enough, this morning Tommasino came to our rooms at nine o'clock. And brought me a poem. He rode along beside us, when we left, as far as the city gate, and stood waving good-by to us, until our carriage was out of sight.

W.

the best of friends

CROME

Dear Nannerl—

Easter Sunday was ten days ago, but we got here four days before *that*, on the Wednesday of Holy Week, so we have seen *everything!*

I have been writing a symphony in my spare time, and Papa has been copying it out himself—for fear that if he were to send it to the copyists, they would steal it and sell it before we ever had a chance to make any money from it.

The trip from Florence was cold and long and tiresome. The inns were terrible and we could hardly get anything decent to eat. No meat at all, because of Lent. The fish smelled awful. So all we ate was broccoli and eggs, eggs and broccoli, for days and days.

Nannerl, you would love Rome! The sky is so bright and clear and blue. Pale blue. And rising up into it are the seven

hills of Rome, covered with old, old ruins, and with tall, black, pointed cypresses, and little flat-topped Roman pines. Ever since what happened to me on Good Friday, I have been invited over and over again to all the great houses and palaces in Rome, to meet princesses, cardinals, and dukes, amidst such great families as the Braccianos, the Chigis, and the Barbarinis.

And so now, you will ask, what happened on Good Friday? And (since you ask) I will tell you, cara sorella mia!

But I must start at the beginning.

We got to Rome on April 11, the Wednesday of Holy Week, in the midst of a terrible rain and thunderstorm that sounded like 1,000 cannon going off. Papa was sure we would be killed by lightning.

As soon as we were settled in our rooms in the inn we went across the Tiber River to St. Peter's, because we wanted to be in time to see the pope perform his holy offices. (Papa says the Holy Father was born Lorenzo Ganganelli, but now, of course, he is His Holiness Pope Clement XIV.)

Now, as you may know, on the Wednesday, Thursday, and Friday of Holy Week, a service is offered at St. Peter's which is called the Tenebrae. (Papa says that is Latin, for "shadows," Horseface.)

And during the Tenebrae, the pope and the cardinals are there, in the Sistine Chapel. The chapel is very dark, because there are only thirteen candles burning—one for Christ and one for each of his twelve disciples. The cardinals are not wearing red, as you would suppose. Because for these special services during Holy Week, they wear purple—for they are in mourning for the death of Christ. And the pope himself does not wear his triple crown nor his gorgeous robes. He removes everything but a simple white smock, for he is in mourning too.

In front of the altar is a bier, draped in a purple pall, representing the dead Christ. Against the far wall, you can see the souls in torment, where Michelangelo painted his *Last Judgment*. And overhead, high on the Sistine ceiling, you can see his fresco of God the Father, in His white beard and robe, His hand outstretched, having just touched Adam, to bring to life the first man who ever lived on earth.

There, with the thirteen candles burning, and the purple-clad cardinals and the pope lying prostrate at the foot of the cross, and God the Father floating overhead—then and there the choir begins to sing the Miserere.

The words are in Latin, and they are taken, as I suppose you know, from the fifty-first psalm in the Old Testament:

> Have mercy upon me, O God,
> according to thy loving-kindness,
> according unto the multitude
> of thy tender mercies,
> blot out my transgressions. . . .

Wash me thoroughly from mine iniquity,
and cleanse me from my sin. . . .

For I acknowledge my transgressions:
and my sin is ever before me. . . .

It is a most incredibly solemn and holy moment.

That is when—without any organ or any other instrument to support them—the thirty-two voices of the papal choir begin to chant the psalm—the Miserere—as it was written by Gregorio Allegri more than a hundred years ago.

I am told that a few copies of this wonderful music have been made, but nobody ever seems to have been able to duplicate it in performance anywhere but here in the Sistine Chapel, in Rome.

Papa had told me all about it, in advance, so I was ready. And I began to memorize it, very carefully, note for note, so that I could slip it all into my memory bag.

But the best part is *this*, Nannerl. As they sing the Miserere, one by one the thirteen candles on the altar are snuffed out. The chapel gets darker and darker, until there is only one central light left burning.

You can barely make out God the Father, floating overhead, and the Holy Father, prostrate at the foot of the cross.

Then the last light is gone, and the music is at an end.

The last candle has not been extinguished—for the light of Christ never entirely abandons us—but it has been hidden

behind the altar. And it seems as if the end of the world
has come, until that last candle flame reappears, at last, and
the other twelve candles are lighted, from it, again.

Well, when the service was over and Papa and I were back
at our inn, I wrote the whole Miserere down on paper, note

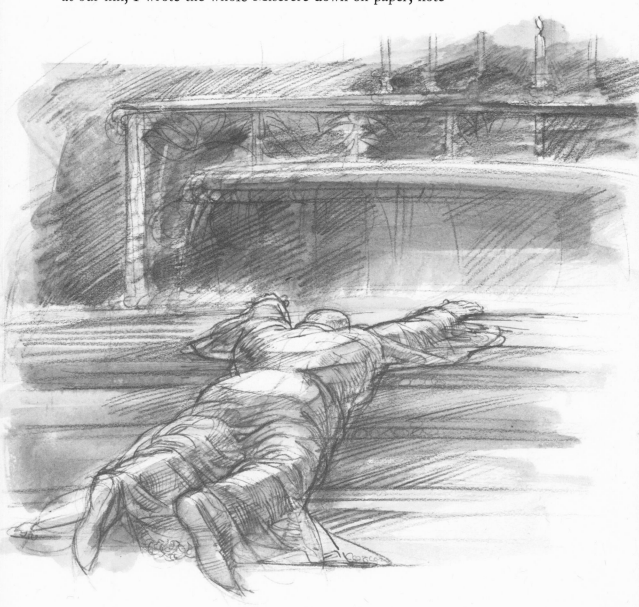

for note, from memory. Papa didn't believe I could really do it, but I assured him I had, and that I didn't think I'd made too many mistakes.

The next day—Maundy Thursday—we went back to the Vatican.

This is the day, you know, when the pope washes the feet of twelve poor men, brought in from off the streets. After the foot-washing, he serves them a meal at his table, in memory of the Last Supper, when Christ washed the feet of his disciples, and said to them:

> Little children, yet a little while I am with you.
> . . . Whither I go ye cannot come, so now I say
> to you . . . . A new commandment I give unto
> you: That ye love one another; as I have loved
> you that ye also love one another.

Then, after the Holy Father serves the meal, he and the cardinals go into the Sistine Chapel, with all the thousands of worshipers, and the service of the Tenebrae is repeated, and the Miserere sung again.

I had forgotten to bring my copy of the music on Thursday, but luckily the Miserere is also sung again, for the last time, on Good Friday.

And on Good Friday, I smuggled the score into the chapel in my hat, and followed it, note for note, from my manuscript, making a few corrections here and there.

Later we met Cardinal Pallavicini, and when Papa told him what I'd been able to do, he was amazed. He and some other Romans wanted to know if I could sing the Miserere. So I did. And they were amazed all over again.

Aren't they foolish, Nannerl? I don't know *where* it comes from. I suppose God gives me the ability—as Papa says.

But you know, sometimes I think the loveliest instrument of all is a massed chorus of voices. Be sure to remind me, Nannerl, to write something grand, someday, for a massed chorus! Something solemn and impressive. Like the Miserere.

Well, when you next hear from us, we'll be in Naples. That is if the bandits don't get us. Papa says the bandits between Rome and Naples are worse than *anywhere* else in Italy.

Tell Mama not to worry. Papa and I are both well, and we send you both 10,000 kisses.

From your little wunderkind,
Wolferl

P.S. I think I told you I was writing a symphony?

P.P.S. On the Saturday before Easter, Papa took me to the Vatican again to pay homage to St. Peter's statue. So many people have kissed his foot that his bronze toe is nearly worn away. Your little Wolferl is so short that he couldn't reach it, and so Papa had to lift me up!

W.

NAPLES

Dear old Nannerl-the-Horseface—

We've been here since May 14, and only received our first letter here in Naples from you and Mama today. We're so far south now that it takes two weeks for mail from Salzburg to reach us.

Papa and I laughed when we read that you and Mama were sure I had committed a sin or a crime when I copied down the music of the Miserere on Good Friday! Did you *really* think I would be punished? The Holy Father himself knew all about it, Nannerl. He wasn't angry at all. He even congratulated Papa, for having such a remarkable son! So you and Mama can stop worrying about *that* right now!

How I wish you were with us in Naples! Papa says that Naples and Constantinople are supposed to have the two loveliest situations in all Europe. And the Neapolitans are very proud of their city. You know what they say? *"Vedi Napoli e poi muori."* (And *that*, Horseface, means: "See Naples, and die.")

Well, I've seen it. But I don't feel like dying for a long, long time! Tra-la-la-liera! Tra-la-la-liera!

But it is so very beautiful, Nannerl, that I wish you and Mama could see it, too. The weather is always warm and sunny. The boxwood and the myrtles and the laurel are in bloom. There are palm trees, and fountains, and whole gardens filled with orange and lemon trees. Their white flowers and their golden fruit hang in the glossy green leaves, together, and their perfume is deliciously heavy and sweet.

The sea is a heavenly blue color, and so is the sky. The lovely bay curves gently in a large half-circle, and there to the south is the cone of Vesuvius. Papa and I are sorry to report that the volcano is not presently spitting fire and lava and ashes, in honor of the Mighty Musical Mozarts, but confines itself to a thin, harmless plume of smoke that trails westward across the bay, into the red and gold sunset.

Since Naples is so beautiful and the weather is so lovely, everybody lives outdoors as much as he possibly can. The streets are always swarming with people of every degree, and there is so much to see! Naples is like a huge outdoor Carnival that never ends. Like a wonderful comic opera that goes on day after day, with no finale.

There are always crowds standing about, laughing and

chattering, watching and listening. Maybe it's a friar, standing on a barrel, preaching to the crowd. Or a quack doctor selling love potions, or cures for jealousy, or charms against the evil eye. Or a Punch and Judy show, with puppets beating each other over the head with sticks, joking and cursing and shrieking and throwing the baby, bundled up in white lace, out of the window into the street below! Or there may be live actors, dressed up as Harlequin and Columbina and Pantalone and Pulcinello, acting a comedy on an open platform in the square. Or a tightrope walker, turning frighten-

ing somersaults and cartwheels, high, high up, overhead.

Because everyone lives in the streets, Naples is like one huge, outdoor room, where everything imaginable takes place, right out under the open sky.

Here is what you see them selling in the markets: broccoli and tomatoes and eggplant and pyramids of grapes and chestnuts and oranges and lemons and apples and pears. And baskets of figs and nuts and melons, twined with sprigs of rosemary.

Cows are led from door to door for milking, and pigs and goats and chickens run loose in the streets.

Men stand on the corners with huge tubs of ice-cold lemonade, dipping up cool drinks and selling them to passers-by. Others fry little cakes in hot fat, and serve them piping hot. Or, if you prefer, there is spaghetti and cheese and oil, which you dip up out of the pot, toss your head back, and eat with your fingers.

Down at the edge of the bay the fishing boats come back from their daily trips to sea, to a district called Santa Lucia. And there the fishermen unload carp and bass and flounder and shellfish of all kinds, which they call *frutta di mare,* which means, Horseface, "fruit of the sea." And right there at the water's edge, tables are set up where Papa and I have eaten great platters of fried prawns and scallops and shrimps and mussels and crabs—all golden brown and hot and delicious.

pasta, al fresco!

56

In the open streets, in front of their stalls, you may see carpenters building cabinets; women cutting cheeses on marble slabs, or weaving lace, or sewing artificial silk flowers; butchers plucking chickens and stringing sausages; barbers shaving customers, and frizzing wigs with hot curling irons; and blacksmiths shoeing horses.

Everybody who isn't laughing seems to be singing. Papa said to me, "As we go farther and farther south, in Italy, Wolferl, the people seem to grow poorer and poorer. But they seem to love music more, too." And that is so. There are many beggars in the streets here. And cripples. And idlers who are called *lazzaroni* by the Italians. (That's a word that can mean "rascals," or "beggars," or "thieves," Horseface, depending on the circumstances.)

But though the Neapolitans may be poor, they seem to love singing more than they love anything else in the world. For here it is that beautiful voices seem to grow and flower and spread their perfume as sweetly and naturally as the cream-white flowers of the lemon trees do, in their thickets of glossy green leaves.

Naples is filled with music. The fishermen sing. The barbers sing. The lace-makers sing. The lazzaroni sing. And, of course, at the San Carlo opera house, you have come to the very inner heart of the murmuring rose, where you may become as drunk as you please on golden melody.

Papa says the San Carlo is the biggest opera house in

Europe. And it is shaped something like a rose, too, with its six tiers of boxes, glittering with candles and mirrors and filled with ladies wearing jewels. The ceiling is painted with angels and nymphs, and the stage itself is huge. Papa says they've had real elephants on stage, at San Carlo, in some opera or other—I forget which. And the acoustics are glorious.

The uproar inside the San Carlo is even worse than the uproar in the opera house in Milan. People eating, gambling, talking, laughing—until the arias begin. And then complete silence, until they are sung. Then loud, long bursts of applause and "bravos!" and "bravissimi!" and "bravas!" while the soprano blushes and curtsies, and the basso bows. Oh, Nannerl, can there be anything more beautiful and exciting than the opera? Your foolish brother Wolferl doesn't think so!

We've seen a number of operas here at the San Carlo. And this past week we have attended the rehearsals for Signor Jomelli's new opera, *Armida Abbandonata,* which opened tonight.

I like Jomelli (though the music of his opera is a little old-fashioned) but Papa has a grudge against him, because he says Jomelli somehow kept me from giving a concert for the duke of Württemberg, seven years ago, when we were in Stuttgart. I don't remember any of the details, but Papa never forgets anything like that, as you know.

Jomelli's opera was a success, and King Ferdinand and Queen Maria Carolina were there tonight, in the royal box.

Papa and I wore our new summer clothes for the occasion. My coat is flame-colored (*colore di fuoco*, as the Italians say) moiré silk, trimmed with silver lace and lined with blue silk; Papa's is dark red silk, *also* trimmed with silver lace, and lined with apple-green.

When the king and queen come to the opera they are accompanied by a crowd of courtiers, and troops of mounted dragoons that nearly trample the people crowding the narrow streets. Queen Maria Carolina is our Empress Maria Theresa's daughter—one of her sixteen children. She is tall and rather beautiful.

King Ferdinand is dark and stocky, and rather doltish. He is much shorter than Maria Carolina. They say he has to stand on a footstool, when he's in the royal box at the opera, so he'll look taller than the queen!

Jomelli was frantic because he thought their majesties would be an hour or two late for the performance—as they often are. And, of course, the opera can't begin without them. But they were only twenty minutes late, and so Signor Jomelli was at last able to breathe again, and conducted his opera in triumph, from the harpsichord.

And this winter, Nannerl, I shall do likewise, in Milan, when my own opera is produced! Think of it! This Christmas, in Milan!

Papa knows a lot of funny stories about King Ferdinand that he is saving to tell Mama when he gets home. The king is quite an oaf, and he's rather afraid of the mobs of beggars in the streets here, and pays a fixed sum of money every month to their chief, so that they won't make any trouble. Maybe that's why people call him the Lazzarone King!

Papa says his majesty hates music and loves nothing so

much as hunting wolves. He keeps chickens and goats and pigs and monkeys in cages in his palace, they say, just for the fun of letting them loose and chasing them about! He must be very odd, indeed. And Papa says he likes to slip spoonfuls of jam and marmalade into the gloves and pockets of his guests—as a joke! Can you imagine?

Papa is hoping that I will be able to give a concert for their Neapolitan majesties, but so far none has been arranged. Perhaps it is just as well, this way. I don't think I would like to try playing my sonatas at the harpsichord, with my fingers all sticky with jam!

I have heard several good comic operas by Piccini and Paisiello, and have given a few concerts. Count Kaunitz, the Austrian ambassador, has had a reception and concert for us, where I played. And on May 16, Papa and I went to a great ball given by the French ambassador, in honor of the dauphin of France—who was married that day to our Austrian archduchess, Marie Antoinette, at Versailles.

But *I* was supposed to marry little Marie Antoinette, Nannerl, don't you remember? Ah, well, I suppose I shall have to find another princess.

Tra-la-la-liera! Tra-la-la-liera! I refuse to be downhearted.

The Marchesa Tannucci, wife of the prime minister, lent her carriage to Papa and me last week, so we could go sightseeing to Pompeii and Herculaneum and Vesuvius.

And Papa says to be sure to tell you and Mama that if I had not already been given the scrittura to write an opera for Milan, I could have had one from Bologna, or Rome, or Naples, for I have received offers to write operas from each of those cities as well. But, of course, I had to turn the others down.

I hope you can read my writing. Papa says it is terrible!

I sleep a lot here, and so I did in Rome, for the hot weather in Italy is very tiring. Nevertheless, Papa says he has never seen me more lively—except for those few days in Rome when I had the toothache.

But I must tell you how superstitious they are in Naples. A few days ago I gave a concert at the Conservatorio della Pietà—and while I was playing a theme and improvised variations on the harpsichord, Papa heard them murmuring in the audience, "The ring! The ring!"

At first he didn't know what they meant. (I was wearing my diamond ring on the little finger of my right hand, as I always do.) Then Papa realized that they thought it was the *ring* that was giving my hands some sort of magic power.

So Papa let me finish the performance, and after the applause was over, he came up and made me take the ring off, and told me to begin playing my variations, all over again. Well, I did. And when I was through the second time, the applause was so thunderous I thought the roof would fall in! Isn't that surprising? They really thought it might have been the ring that helped me play!

Now I must tell you about the Molo, and then I must stop. Do you know what a mole is, Horseface? Not the *animal*, stupid. The *other* kind of mole.

Well, a mole is like a breakwater. And down on the Bay of Naples there is a huge, broad, flat-topped stone breakwater, reaching out into the blue water, and it's called the Molo.

And in the afternoon and evening, people stroll back and forth on top of the Molo, enjoying the cool sea breezes. And the nobles drive their carriages out onto the Molo—the most fashionable time of all being Friday afternoons.

Well, late last Friday afternoon, when Papa and I were on the Molo, Queen Maria Carolina came driving out in her open carriage. When the warships in the harbor saw her, they fired their cannon, in salute.

And when she saw Papa and Wolferl, Queen Maria Carolina smiled and bowed to us! What do you think of that!

I wish you could see a sunset on the Bay of Naples, Nannerl, with the stars coming out in the heavens overhead. And smell the scent of the sea on the evening breeze. And see the carriages, with their torches alight, slowly driving up and down the Molo. Somewhere a mandolin begins to play, as a man in a walled garden begins singing to some beautiful signorina, half-hidden on a balcony above. . . . Then comes the scent of the lemon blossoms, and the song of the nightingale drifts through the evening air.

Someday, Nannerl, I swear it, I shall squeeze all of the

happy laughter, all of the colors, all of the music, and all of the perfumes of Naples into one single glorious comic opera. All of them. *All* of them. Tra-la-la-liera! See if I don't! I don't know how I know it, but I *know* it's true!

Tell Mama her Simple Simon son sends her 10,000 kisses.

Your loving brother,
Wolferl

P.S. Tell me, how is Mr. Canary? Does he still sing? And still whistle? Do you know what makes me think of him? There is a canary in our front room *here* in Naples, which makes a noise just like ours at home!

W.

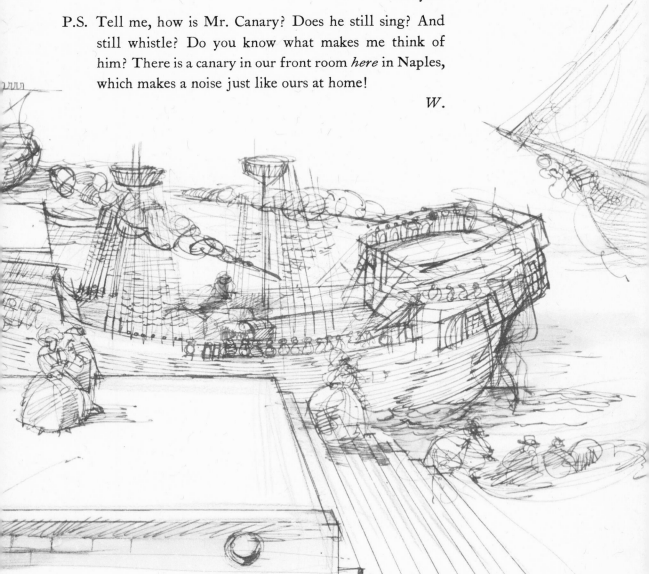

ROME

the Holy Father

July 9, 1770

Cara sorella mia—

We left Naples on June 27, and were here in Rome just twenty-seven hours later. The mail coach simply flew! Papa and I were tired, and Papa was in pain, besides. He didn't want to be delayed by the customs offiicals, so he pretended we were great nobles, and threw a few coins to the soldiers, and they let us pass through without any questions asked.

At our rooms we found your letters, and the portraits of yourselves that you and Mama had painted in Salzburg. Papa and I are very pleased with them!

We laughed when we saw that Mama wanted to know if I had begun writing my opera, yet, for Milan. The answer is no! I have not even begun to think about it. And just as well, too. They have not yet sent me the libretto (that is, the text, Horseface) so I don't even know what it is about,

66

myself. Sometime I must tell you about how operas are composed, in Italy. So much arguing and fighting. You would be amused.

Papa has written you, I know, about how he hurt his leg on the last stage of our journey here, when the carriage sank into some soft sand and nearly overturned. He struck his shin so hard that his leg was badly cut, but he is much better now, though still limping. Tell Mama not to worry. I will look after Papa!

I must tell you, though, that your foolish little brother Wolferl has made such a reputation for himself with his music here in Italy that you may no longer call him Wolferl!

That is right. For on July 8, His Holiness Clement XIV conferred upon me the Order of the Golden Spur, which means that I am now a knight, and a very important fellow. As a result of this, everyone in Rome now calls me "Signor Cavaliere Amadeo," and you must do likewise, Horseface!

Papa says that because of his leg injury, we will not return by way of Florence, as we had planned, but will go instead to Bologna, by way of Loreto and Sinegaglia, on the Adriatic. Since we will not be going to Florence, it means I shall not see my dear friend Tommasino Linley, after all. I must write and tell him. I am sure he will be as disappointed as I am, but with luck we may soon have a chance to meet again, elsewhere.

Papa says I must be sure to tell you and Mama that I

have grown so much in Italy that my shirtsleeves have had to be lengthened, and that I am outgrowing my trousers, as well.

(That is *true*, Nannerl, but I am still so short I look like a little boy. Do you think I'll ever be really tall? I don't. And whoever heard of a stumpy, short little cavalier?)

Not only that, my voice is changing, so I can no longer sing the soprano arias I've composed. It's all very irritating, and hard to understand.

This letter will have to be a short one, as we are leaving Rome tomorrow, and we must get our rest in preparation for the journey.

Papa says to tell Mama he will write her a long letter, as soon as we get to Bologna.

And so, Mademoiselle, *j'ai l'honneur d'être vos très humble serviteur et frère,*

Chevalier Mozart

P.S. (And that's *French*, Horseface, for "I have the honor to be your most humble servant and brother, Wolfgang Mozart, Knight of the Golden Spur.")

CROCE DI BIACCO

Dear Nannerl—

We've been in Bologna since July 20, having stopped to worship at the shrine of the Virgin, in Loreto, on our way here.

Papa's injured leg still troubles him, and I tell him he has become impatient, now that he is gouty and partially bed-ridden. And Papa tells *me* that I am untidier than ever, now that he cannot stand over me and make me be neat. He wrote Mama that I kept my room at the inn in Bologna in a terrible mess, and I'm afraid it was true!

But you should see us now. For now we are living like great lords in Count Pallavicini's beautiful summer home, called Croce di Biacco. We eat off silver dishes here, and sleep on the finest linen. We have two servants to wait on us, a footman and a valet. And my valet is also my *friseur*

(and *that*, Horseface, means that he is somebody who knows how to dress and curl and frizz my wig!)

We are in two lovely, cool rooms on the ground floor, and we take our meals on the terrace, overlooking the garden.

I've gotten to know the young count, Pallavicini's son, quite well indeed. He is most friendly, and takes us out driving in his carriage every afternoon. He is very talented, plays the clavier, speaks German, Italian, and French, and has five or six masters in, to teach him something every day.

We have been eating the most delicious figs and peaches and melons while here, and are lucky indeed to be passing the hottest part of the Italian summer in a retreat as cool and comfortable and shady as this one.

You will also be interested to know, Horseface, that I am studying counterpoint almost daily with Padre Martini. Do you remember my telling you of him? Papa says he is probably the greatest musical scholar in Italy today.

Papa is a bit annoyed that his book, *The Violinist's Handbook*, has never yet been sent to him from Salzburg. He very much wants to hand a copy to Padre Martini. And I think you and Mama are very naughty not to have sent it to him!

Padre Martini belongs to the famous Bologna Philharmonic Academy, as I told you before, and he has invited Papa and me to come to their annual festival, which takes place on August 30. Among other things, a vespers and a high mass will be sung, and we are eager to hear them.

You will also want to tell Mama that we have met an Englishman here named Dr. Charles Burney, who remembered hearing all of us Mighty Musical Mozarts, when we were in London, six years ago. He told Papa that my "precocious and supernatural talent amazed us all in London,

My lessons with Padre Martini

some years ago." He recalled an evening, which I had forgotten, when we had gone to the palace in London to play for King George III and Queen Charlotte. Dr. Burney was there, too, and heard me accompany the queen in an aria which she sang. And then I apparently sat at the harpsichord with Johann Christian Bach—who was then in London—and played a sonata with him, he and I playing alternate phrases. I really don't remember any of this, but Dr. Burney told Papa I was such a little boy that I jumped down from the harpsichord when a cat came into the room, and could hardly be persuaded to stop petting her, and be brought back to my music. He also said that later that evening, I rode a stick about the room, pretending it was a hobbyhorse. What a silly little wunderkind this Wolferl must have been!

Do you remember things like this, from our Grand Tour of Europe, Nannerl, when we went to Germany and Holland and Belgium, and to Paris to meet the king and queen of France, and to London to play for the king and queen of England? You ought to, better than I do, for you're five years older. And I was only seven or eight at the time.

Dr. Burney has come to Bologna to meet Padre Martini, because *both* of them are writing histories of music, and they have much to discuss together. Both of these learned gentlemen assure Papa that the world may expect to hear great things of me.

"I hear the boy has been much admired in Rome and

Naples," said Dr. Burney, and Padre Martini said it was so.

"Don't forget Tommasino Linley," I reminded them, for Tommasino and I are often mentioned, these days, as the twin wonders of the musical world.

"Yes. Yes," said Padre Martini. "We expect to hear great things of *both* you boys," and Dr. Burney and Papa agreed.

Last of all, you and Mama will be interested to know that I have finally heard from Milan about my opera. They have decided to have me write the music for a work that has been set to music once before—a libretto called *Mithridate, King of Pontus*. Papa says that the play on which it is based was written about a hundred years ago by the great French dramatist, Racine. But this libretto is by an Italian named Cigna-Santi, and Papa says it is not bad at all.

(I was a little disappointed, because I had hoped to be sent a libretto by the great poet, Metastasio. But, tra-la-la-liera! Tra-la-la-liera! I refuse to be downhearted.)

We think that Santorini and Ettore may be singing in my opera, but it's not certain yet, and until I know for sure, there is not much point to start composing. (I'll write you more about this one day, Horseface. It's sad, and funny, and fascinating, and maddening, all at once.)

I only wish I knew who my prima donna was going to be! Give my love to Mama, and keep a lot for yourself.

Your simpleton brother,
Wolferl

MILAN

November 3, 1770

Dear Nannerl—

This has to be a short letter, because I am hard at work on the connecting passages of my opera (not the arias, Horse-face, but the *other* parts, called the recitatives). And my fingers ache so that I can hardly hold my pen.

We got to Milan on October 18, having had to delay our journey for a day in Parma, waiting for the floodwaters of the river to fall, so that we could get across it on the ferry.

I am happy to be able to tell you that before we left Bologna, a copy of Papa's *Violinist's Handbook* arrived, and he was able to present it to Padre Martini. How happy that made Papa! Now he and Martini are the best of friends.

Something nice happened to me, too, before I left Bologna. Padre Martini invited me to take the examination to be admitted as a full-fledged composer in the Bologna Phil-

77

harmonic Academy. Now, the academy has never admitted anybody younger than twenty, before this, so it is a great honor (Papa says) that they let a fourteen year old boy—like me—take the test at all.

Well, this is what happened. On October 9, I had to appear at the hall of the Bologna Philharmonic, where three old men gave me an antiphon to arrange for four-part singing. (An antiphon, Horseface, is a psalm that is sung, responsively, by two choruses.) An old beadle locked me into a room, and in less than an hour I was finished.

Padre Martini told Papa that many people taking this examination take three hours to finish a three line antiphon.

My unanimous election

Anyway, I finished much sooner than *that*, and I was elected to the academy by a unanimous vote of the members. So now, my dear sister, you must call me what the Italians call me—Signor Cavaliere Filarmonico. (You see, Horse-face, my titles grow longer and longer, for now I am not only a Knight of the Golden Spur, but also a member of the celebrated Bologna Philharmonic Academy!)

My toothache has come back to plague me, now that I am ready to begin the hard work of writing my opera. But Papa says, "Do not be discouraged, Wolferl. This great undertaking is nearly over. And we shall nibble our way through these unavoidable annoyances."

I hope he is right. Papa says I have become so serious that he wishes you and Mama would send me some jokes, so that I could laugh again.

Thanks to you and Mama for the greetings you sent me on my name day, on October 31. And, dear Nannerl, you and Mama must now pray that my opera may go well. For then we could be together, and all of us would be happy again.

You know what a great chatterbox I am, Nannerl, so you will understand how difficult it is for me to bring this letter to a close. I must not stay up late, though, otherwise I will have no strength left for working on my opera.

A hundred thousand kisses for you and Mama,

from your busy brother,
Wolferl

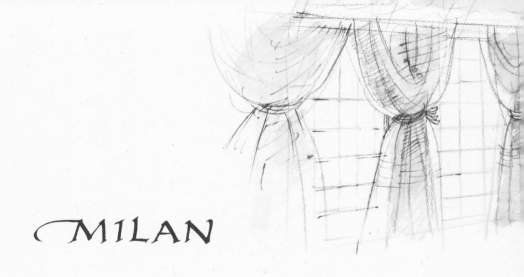

CMILAN

December 15, 1770

Dear Nannerl—

I don't think I told you about our rooms. We are living close to the theater, in two large rooms. The living room has three large windows and a fireplace. And our bed is about nine feet wide!

As soon as my opera is performed here, Papa says we will take a little trip to Venice, to see the Carnival, and then home to Salzburg! (Papa says please to ask Herr Hagenauer where we should rent rooms in Venice.)

I can hardly wait to see you and Mama. But my opera must be a success, first, or else we will have wasted all our time in Italy for nothing.

When something is a success, here, they say that it has risen *"alle stelle"*—right up to the stars. So that is what you must hope for my opera, Horseface. You must hope it will go alle stelle.

Papa will not allow me to tire myself too much, so he permits me to compose only in the mornings, before lunch. Then we go walking in the afternoon. And rehearsals are in the evening.

Did Papa tell you what trouble we have had? *Almost* had, I should say, for everything is all right now.

The first day the prima donna came to rehearsals, someone went to her and said that she should sing only the *old* music for the opera (which was originally written by an Italian). Because I was nothing but a barbarian German, and besides I was a mere child who could not possibly write a good opera, or conduct one successfully.

I have never seen Papa so angry! You should have seen the letter he wrote to Padre Martini in Bologna, telling him all about it.

Anyway, Papa and I went straight to Signora Antonia Bernasconi—she is the prima donna, who sings the role of Princess Aspasia in my opera. And we talked to her and to

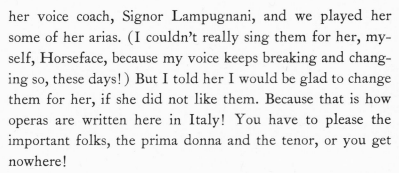

her voice coach, Signor Lampugnani, and we played her some of her arias. (I couldn't really sing them for her, myself, Horseface, because my voice keeps breaking and changing so, these days!) But I told her I would be glad to change them for her, if she did not like them. Because that is how operas are written here in Italy! You have to please the important folks, the prima donna and the tenor, or you get nowhere!

But everything turned out for the best, for Signora Bernasconi was beside herself with delight with my music, and said the arias I had written suited her exactly. And so did her coach, Signor Lampugnani, who now praises my work everywhere he goes.

Santorini, the leading man, did not get here until the very end of November. And I did not dare begin composing anything for him until after I had heard his voice. For it would have been a waste of time to write something unsuitable for him. And this has meant that I have had to be busy writing arias for him, at the same time I have been rehearsing the orchestra! (This isn't as bad as it may sound, though, for quite a few of the melodies for his arias were already safely stowed away, in the depths of my memory bag.)

The composing of operas here, in Italy, Nannerl, is a mad, mad business! You wouldn't believe half of what goes on, unless you saw it for yourself.

Papa says that the orchestra rehearsals are going well, and that the singers are good. Maestro Sammartini has heard my opera, and likes it, but Papa says, "Don't get your hopes up too high, Wolferl. An opera is like a lottery. You need to be lucky, in order to win!"

And so I hope I shall be lucky, on December 26, Nannerl. For that is our opening night. Tell Mama that my opera opens the day after her birthday, which is on Christmas Day.

So pray for me and wish me luck.

Your ink-stained brother,
Wolferl

P.S. There is one more lucky sign. Ever since the first or-chestra rehearsal, the music copyist has been walking around with his face all smiles. Now, when an opera goes well, the music copyist sometimes makes more money than the composer himself, because the copyist has the right to sell copies of the arias to anyone who wants to buy them. So if the copyist looks happy, maybe we are going to have a *real* success, after all!

P.P.S. During all our rehearsals, Papa stands at the very back of the house, near the entrance doors. In a few days, the tailor is going to start making me a new suit for opening night. It will be scarlet, lined with blue, trimmed with gold braid. Picture me wearing that, on opening night, Nannerl. Conducting the or-chestra from my seat at the harpsichord. . . .

alle stelle!

MILAN

December 27, 1770

Dear old Nannerl—

God be praised, everyone applauded my opera!

We had the good luck we hoped we'd have. And Papa says it's a success, alle stelle!

On the 26th, when the curtain fell, people shouted *"Evviva il Maestrino!"* ("Long live the little composer!") And during the performance Signora Bernasconi had to repeat one of her arias—because so many cried out *"Fuora!"*—"Again!" And this is something that almost *never* happens at an opening night in Milan.

How I wish that you and Mama could have been there to hear it all.

Tickets are selling well in advance, and Papa says we shall certainly have more than twenty performances. And the copyist is smiling more broadly than ever.

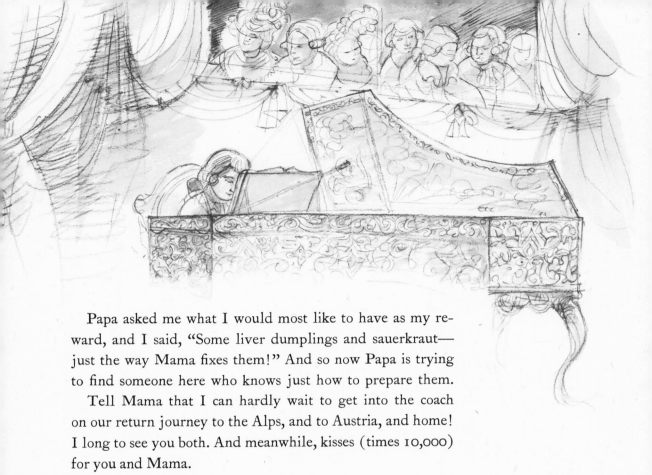

Papa asked me what I would most like to have as my reward, and I said, "Some liver dumplings and sauerkraut—just the way Mama fixes them!" And so now Papa is trying to find someone here who knows just how to prepare them.

Tell Mama that I can hardly wait to get into the coach on our return journey to the Alps, and to Austria, and home! I long to see you both. And meanwhile, kisses (times 10,000) for you and Mama.

Your homesick brother,
Wolferl

P.S. Here is a riddle, Horseface. What is the same on each end, and double in the middle? Answer: the year 1771. And *that* is the year when Wolferl will be coming home, to Salzburg.

W.

About This Story

For those who wish to know a bit more about Mozart, his family, and his times:

Anna Maria Pertl ("Mama" 1720–1778) married Leopold Mozart on November 21, 1747. She and Leopold were thought to be the best-looking couple in Salzburg. They had seven children, all of whom died in infancy except for Nannerl and Wolferl. Frau Mozart died of a fever, in Paris, in 1778; she had accompanied her son there on one of his concert tours, and Wolfgang had to write the sad news of her death to his father, in Salzburg.

Leopold Mozart ("Papa" 1719–1787) survived his wife by nine years, and lived to see his son compose two of his greatest operas—*The Marriage of Figaro*, and *Don Giovanni*—dying only four years before Wolfgang himself. For most of his adult life, Leopold lived in Salzburg where he was employed as a court musician—first by the kindly Archbishop Schrattenbach, and after that prelate's death in 1772, by the boorish and troublesome Archbishop Hieronymus, Count Colloredo. Leopold was one of the best teachers of the violin in his day, in all Europe. He devoted much of his life to fostering the career and genius of his remarkable son.

87

Giovanni Battista Martini (1706–1784) the kindly, learned padre whom the Mozarts met in Bologna, owned a vast music library of 17,000 volumes, and maintained cordial relations with scholars and rulers, including Frederick the Great, Frederick William II of Prussia, Princess Maria Antonia of Saxony, and Pope Clement XIV. Grove's *Dictionary of Music and Musicians* states: "It is difficult to think without emotion of the warm welcome which he, the most learned and one of the oldest musicians of his country, gave to Mozart when he visited Bologna in 1770 as a boy of fourteen."

Thomas Linley, Jr., (1756–1778) was one of the many gifted children of the English singing master and composer, Thomas Linley, Sr., of Bath. Another member of this highly talented musical and theatrical family was Tommasino's marvelously beautiful elder sister, Elizabeth (1754–1792), a soprano, who eloped under highly romantic circumstances from Bath in the spring of 1773, to be secretly married to the dashing young Irish playwright, Richard Brinsley Sheridan, who later wrote *The School for Scandal*. Thomas Linley's promising career was cut short when he drowned in a tragic boating accident, at the age of twenty-two. Long afterwards, in Vienna, Mozart spoke of him and lamented his early death. The two friends never saw one another again after their first meeting in Florence.

Maria Anna Mozart ("Nannerl" 1751–1830) was five years older than her brother, and a very accomplished pianist and singer in her own right. As children, she and Wolferl amazed many of the courts of Europe, performing before the emperor and empress of Austria, the king and queen of France, and the king and queen of England, as well as many lesser rulers in Germany and the Low Countries. Her brother was not quite thirty-six years old when he died, but Nannerl lived to be an old lady of seventy-nine, dying in Salzburg, in 1830. In 1784 Nannerl married a noble of the Holy Roman Empire, Baron von Berchtold zu Sonnenburg.

Wolfgang Amadeus Mozart ("Wolferl" January 27, 1756—December 5, 1791) was probably the greatest musical genius the world has ever seen. In 1782 he married Constanze Weber, a singer, and later became the father of two sons, Karl and Franz. (After his death, Mozart's widow married again. Constanze's second husband was a Dane named Georg Niklaus von Nissen. The Nissens lived in Copenhagen, and Georg wrote a biography of Mozart, which was published in Leipzig in 1828.) Despite the acclaim he had received as a child prodigy and a youth, during all his adult life Mozart was poor and overworked, and often ill and in debt. But the force of his genius was strong enough to overcome all these worldly difficulties and sorrows, for in his thirty-five brief years of life he wrote hundreds and hundreds of incomparable works of art, containing some of the most joyous melodies ever invented. A catalogue of his works by a scholar named Köchel lists 626 items of Mozart's composition, including 23 operas, more than 40 symphonies, more than 60 sonatas, more than 30 concertos, 30 string quartets, more than 100 religious works, and hundreds of shorter instrumental and vocal pieces. The work of twenty lifetimes, in half a lifetime's span!

None of the letters in these pages was actually written by Mozart. But in writing this book, I have made extensive use of a number of Mozart biographies, together with the fascinating *Letters of Mozart and His Family*, edited by Emily Anderson. So I think it is fair to say that I have invented very little which had no basis in fact, in the records, and have essentially recast and rephrased many of the recorded thoughts and observations of Leopold Mozart, and of his unbelievably gifted son, Wolfgang.

For the Mozarts did indeed travel through Italy (December 12, 1769—March 28, 1771) accomplishing the amazing feats recounted here; and they discussed these events in hundreds of letters written (for the most part by Papa Leopold) to Frau Mozart and Nannerl, in Salzburg.

The Italy through which they traveled was still the great fountainhead of European operatic music, though it must not be forgotten that many of the greatest German geniuses had already changed the course of musical history. Johann Sebastian Bach had died in 1750; and Georg Friederich Handel in 1759; while Franz Joseph Haydn (1732–1809) and Christoph Willibald von Gluck (1714–1787) were still vigorously composing in Vienna— though Ludwig von Beethoven was not to be born until that very year—1770—in Bonn.

Though anyone deeply interested in music or painting was eager to study in Italy, that land was not yet a unified nation in the 18th century. France controlled certain areas; Austria owned all of Lombardy, in the north; the Pope ruled various portions of central Italy; and all the south (Naples and Sicily), though called The Kingdom of the Two Sicilies, was nevertheless wholly controlled by Spain: King Charles of Spain was the father of King Ferdinand, the Neapolitans' "Lazzarone King." And Italy was to remain fragmented until 1870—exactly 100 years after Mozart's visit.

As for Mozart himself, it is difficult to know what to say! No brief note—not even a long, scholarly biography—can explain a genius as incandescent as his. I have told here some of the most important events of just a single year in his life—when he was a young boy of fourteen. It was an important and fascinating year, for it saw him compose his first really successful full-length opera. And what he learned from writing *Mithridate, Rè di Ponto*, and what he learned from the multitudes of musicians he met, and from Italy itself, no doubt contributed in some degree to his becoming the greatest composer of operas who ever lived.

Yet nobody who has heard his later opera—*Idomeneo, King of Crete*, 1781; *The Abduction from the Seraglio*, 1772; *The Marriage of Figaro*, 1786; *Don Giovanni*, 1787; *Così fan Tutte*, 1790; *The Magic Flute*, 1791—can quite understand how any human being was able to compose melodies so heavenly. The flutes laugh at the words of the libretto; the strings weep; men in black Italian capes stride about, swaggering in the music itself; brilliantly feathered, winged creatures—half-human, and half-spirit—sing arias sparkling with the notes of silver bells; and the dizzying vocal acrobatics of the singers may remind us of the tight-rope performers turning somersaults high up over the streets of Naples. So Italy may have had something to do with it all. But where did those *melodies* come from?

Not from Italy—for they came straight from the heart and brain of Johann Chrysostom Wolfgang Amadeus Mozart ("Chrysostom" means "mouth of gold," while "Amadeus" means "beloved of God") and we shall probably never hear their equal again.

In hunting for descriptions of Italian carnivals, and of the street life of Naples and Rome, I turned to accounts written by two German travelers in Italy—Augustus von Kotzebue (who was there during the years 1804–05) and Johann Wolfgang von Goethe (who traveled there in 1786–88). They told me much about masks and confetti and fireworks and lazzaroni that I needed to know. But best of all, when I began to regret the fact that there might never again be anyone else like Mozart, I found a paragraph in Goethe's *Italian Journey* which told me a great deal about that great writer's view of history, which I would like to quote here:

"The observation that all greatness is transitory should not make us despair; on the contrary, the realization that the past was great should stimulate us to create something of consequence ourselves, which, even when in its turn, it has fallen in ruins, may continue to inspire our descendants to a noble activity, such as our ancestors never lacked."

F. N. M.

Bibliography

Acton, Harold, *The Bourbons of Naples*, Methuen, London, 1956.

Anderson, Emily, *Letters of Mozart and His Family*, Macmillan, London, 1938.

Fischer, H. C., and Besch, L., *Life of Mozart*, St. Martin's, New York, 1969.

Goethe, Johann Wolfgang von, *Italian Journey*, Pantheon, New York, 1962.

Haldane, Charlotte, *Mozart*, Oxford University Press, New York, 1960.

Hutton, Edward, *Naples and Campania Revisited*, Hollis & Carter, London, 1958.

Kenyon, Max, *Mozart in Salzburg*, G. P. Putnam's, New York, 1953.

Kerst, Friedrich, *Mozart the Man and the Artist as Revealed by His Own Words*, Heubsch, New York, 1905.

Kotzebue, Augustus von, *Travels Through Italy in the Years 1804–1805*, Richard Phillips, London, 1807.

Sitwell, Sacheverell, *Mozart*, Peter Davies Ltd., London, 1932.

Stendhal (Marie Henri Beyle), using a pseudonym (L. A. C. Bombet), *The Life of Mozart*, bound together with an essay titled *On the Present State of Music in Italy*, Wilkins & Carter, Boston, 1839.

Taine, H., *Italy, Rome and Naples*, Leypoldt & Holt, New York, 1869.

Turner, W. J., *Mozart the Man and His Works*, A. A. Knopf, New York, 1938.

Vaussard, Maurice, *Daily Life in 18th Century Italy*, Macmillan, New York, 1963.

About the Author

F. N. Monjo, raised in Stamford, Connecticut, and a descendant of Spanish fur traders, developed an enthusiastic sense of history through anecdotal tales told to him by his family relating back to Civil War times. "Listening to stories like these brought history alive so vividly for me that I was never able to read it as if it were a mere collection of facts and dates."

After graduating from Columbia University, Mr. Monjo became a book editor specializing in children's literature. Utilizing his editorial skills, his lively sense of history, his understanding of children's literature, and his humanist approach, Mr. Monjo has written fourteen popular books for young readers. He lives in Manhattan with his wife, who is a first-grade teacher, and their four children.

About the Illustrators

Don Bolognese and Elaine Raphael were married a year after their graduation from Cooper Union Art School, where they met. For many years they worked together as a team, using their particular knowledge of calligraphy, book design, and illustration techniques to produce children's books of the highest quality, many of which were honored with awards for graphic design. Today they are pursuing individual careers, but the story of the boy Mozart brought them together again as a team, journeying to Italy for study sketches of authentic backgrounds. The result is a superb artists' view of historic fact. Don Bolognese and Elaine Raphael live on a farm in Vermont and also keep a studio in New York City, both of which they share with their two daughters and a female cat named Hercules.

About This Book

The art work for *Letters to Horseface* was done in crayon pencil and pen and ink on handmade paper. The display type was hand-lettered, using a broad-nibbed calligraphy pen. The front matter was set in Janson and the text and back matter in Caslon Old Face. The book was printed by offset and is bound in cloth over boards.